AUTHOR:-
EDYTA
MYDLOWSKA

WALK A WHILE WITH ME

A collection of poetries

<u>DISCLAIMER</u>

This book is a work of poetry.

Our editors have tried their best to edit the write ups and make sure that the write-ups are not plagiarized.

All write-ups in this book are unique work of the writer.

BOOK-O-PEDIA PUBLICATION
(AFFILIATED TO SUBHARAMBH PUBLICATION HOUSE)
KRIYA YOGA ASHRAM LANE, LOKANATH VIHAR
DAMODAR ROAD, PURI, 752001, ODISHA
Email: bookopediapublication@gmail.com
Instagram:
https://www.instagram.com/bookopedia_publication/
COPYRIGHT © EDYTA MYDLOWSKA, 2020

This is a work of poetry. Names, characters, places and incidents are either product of the author's imagination or are used fictitiously and any resemblance to any actual person, living or dead, events or locales is purely coincidental.

"WALK A WHILE WITH ME"
ISBN: 978-93-90528-30-1
POETRY 1st Edition

TYPESETTING BY: SWAGATIKA SAHOO
COVER DESIGN: SUBHAM DEV KUMAR

The opinions/ contents expressed in this book are solely of the author and do not represents the opinions/ standings/ thought of publisher

CONTENTS:

FEW WORDS FROM THE AUTHOR

The writing of this collection of poems was as ragged as imaginary memory of sentimental, afflictive and beautiful journey.
It was a ...."Bizarre Addiction Beyond Ardent Delights Of Origins..."

1. Music World

Seemingly innocent, mentally addictive.
Hello, the music World. Yes, you are afflictive.
In the darkness you give hope and glimpse of sun,
No fear is known to you, you are the one.
Eclipse of the brightest light you spread,
On the edge of emotions you dive, it is a thread.
Not everyone can follow your way,
You are a devotion, sacrifice. You listen, you say ...
Our life is meaningless without your simple touch,
Understand, while present, you leave behind the
eternal scratch.

2. <u>The Sun</u>

When the Sun will come to meet us,
We will stand up on our feet.
We will speak face to face,
As before we could not meet.

When the Sun will rise for more,
Our voices will be lost.
We will scream so loud,
As our paths may never cross.

When our hearts start dancing,
From inside a bright light sings,
We cannot lose rhythm,
While together we will wait for spring.

When the Sun shines on the horizon,
Standing bravely we face the light.

Looking straight in each others eyes,
Searching for the warmest of rays delights.

3. Landscape

Shh... Silence fulfils the space.
There is nothing in this place.
Just this landscape,
A perfect shape.
Wind in the hair,
Fresh breeze in the air.
Sunset. Beauty in the sky.
No fear. Rather desire to fly.
It is frigid outside,
And nowhere to hide.
The shelter is in the soul,
All in harmony and under control.
Covered with snow,
I don't want to go.
Alpine cordillera surrounding me,
Imagine and see...
Breath in. Feel this blank space.
Ice crystals rubbing your face.
And ... there is only silence here,
Which would never disappear.
Frozen tear on the cheek,
And frozen lips – they cannot speak...
Only the voice of wind around,
But in head a hurricane of sound.

I see it in front of my eyes,
It appears and vaporize.
Only whispers in my head,
All words that have been said
If you only knew,
This beautiful view.
Look here, look there....
Look everywhere.
Even far away,
This spirit fulfils my day.

EDYTA MYDLOWSKA

4. Stranger

How about some music making?
Ending all what is heartbreaking.
Life is a perfect mystery,
Life is an art mercenary.
On this land of all lost souls,
Silence I hear. Silence that no one else knows.

Through the misty forest and lust,
Relevant is what became a dust.
And now, you know...
No other place than music I could go.
Generosity is an eternal debt,
Easier to dream and forget,
Rather than wait for what you can't get.

5. New Reality

Knowing that we cannot know,
Imagining presence of a live show,
Seeing life which was unseen,
Slowly overthinking what could have been.
Moments have passed.
Endless questions which never will be asked,
Indistinct thoughts infecting the mind.
Nonetheless, while being quarantined,
Apart from casualty of old days,
Dreams, plans, hopes - We must embrace.
Reload batteries, come back to shape,
Emerge your will to not to escape.
Adapt to new reality, enjoy food, wine, and sun,
Mind the fact that better times are yet to come.

6. Dreamer

Tell me, how many more stars
need to fall from the sky,
Before we understand scars,
and will be able to say goodbye?

Tell me, how many more lies
we will hear from afar,
Until I stop my tearing eyes,
from thinking where we are.

Tell me, it doesn't mean to you,
anything what it means to me.
Maybe then I will move on too,
No more dreams I will see.

Tell me,
that our feelings never crossed.
Let my soul be free,
"Stupid little dreamer, it is all lost ."

7. Imagine

Imagine, see, listen to this,
This sound reminds of a pure bliss.
Wind rubbing the top of the trees,
Birds flying around with such an ease.
Sunshine. Oh, such a beautiful day,
This is the sound of music we play.
Imagine this amusing view,
Look above, the sky is crystal blue.
Smell the freshly cut grass,
This moment will quickly pass...

Just one, abandoned, empty place,
The time does not exist in this space.
Feel the cool breeze,
Enjoy, hear, squeeze.
A heat is catching the skin,
Can you feel it? Rising sun, the day just begin.

It's a beautiful morning, look a the dew,
So innocent, untouched. Amusing view.
Sitting right here,
The sound of nature comes to my ear.
Deep in thoughts, I travel around,
Surrounded by this subtle sound.

EDYTA MYDLOWSKA

"Where is this place, how to get there?"
Hmm, you see... Nowhere.

It's just an imagination, a beautiful paradise,
It's all in music to be precise.
Inside a day-dreamer's mind,
Where all seems real, but what's real is blind.

8. Winter

Ultimately, winter will knock to the door,
You'll see shadows of footsteps on the floor.
Frosty lips would greet a heated heart,
With pleasure, while making deceptive art.

Ultimately, a year would crack another forgotten
bone,
Snow would melt on hard soil, leaving the taste of
spring alone.
You'll listen to the symphony of nightingales,
Discovering sunny, warm, inspiring trails.

And after all, forget you not,
What winter left behind its deepest thought.
The moonlight shall be a guide to all who were left
behind,
Let it lead us to a place where no one will ever lose
their mind.

9. Uncover your heart

In the middle of nowhere,
Lies a treasure that only at night would flare.
Leaves would fall as autumn arrives,
All summer memories will land in archives.
Life... What does that mean?
Why the grass cannot be more green?
Assumptions, theories, 'why?' I ask,
Yet, it's because you must wear a mask...

See... There is life and it is what it is,
Magical, unique, pure beauty bliss.
Imagine, there is enormous light inside,
Shining bright, so bright that you can't hide.
Sun rising just for you each day,
Uncover your heart, life is not so grey ...

10. <u>Dear Life</u>

Meaning is what you've got,
Yet, what's the meaning without a thought?
There is a mystery surrounding you,
Reasons we all take actions too.
Embracing every part of what you give,
Although, sometimes we can't say we fully 'live'.
So please, help me understand – How?
Under all circumstances just now,
Rather than give more answers ahead,
Endless confusion I feel instead?
Smile until your lips dry out
Maintain sane within any doubt
Irrelevant thoughts put aside
Laugh till all chains are untied
Essential energy runs in blood
Do not ever again feel sad
Intuitively, answer to yourself, why?
Are we infinitely aiming for something so high?
Maybe, it's easier to live in a dream,
On the land where happiness is a gleam,
Night gleam of a falling star,
Designed secretly to be a stylish bar.

11. Evening letter

Late evening, good wine,
Waiting for a miracle, simple sign.
Burning cigarette again and again,
The soul attached to chain.

Looking at the old photograph,
And trying to laugh.
Remembering moments from the past,
Wondering why life goes so fast.

Another cigarette, one more glass,
Want to step on greener grass.
And there is nothing to ask for,
Because there is nothing more.

There is no time to regret,
We are flies trapped in the net.
Waiting for a spider to eat us alive,
Without a chance to survive.

Just please, turn down the light,
Keep dreaming, it's alright.
Escape beyond mind, far, far away,
No, no, no truth, not today.

EDYTA MYDLOWSKA

Waited too long for a foolish sign,
Nothing have left from amazing wine.
Time to go, time to leave soon,
Keep searching for the moon.
Only then,
 Time goes back and I'll smoke my cigarette again..

EDYTA MYDLOWSKA

12. Light

I saw it today, saw its light,
Saw a struggle and a fight.
The sunset in front of me,
Disappeared on the horizon of empty sea.
Happy smile, eyes having fun,
I saw it, I saw the Sun.
I dreamt about it, swear I did,
Nothing compares to it.
I cannot explain,
Like a Sun, it repeats all over again.
I saw a beautiful landscape, and yet.
Why did it make me feel upset?

13. Watch

Lightening brightened the sky today,
Origin of a sudden shock.
Obfuscating silence, gustily started to play,
Knocking on stranger's door.
Again and again. New light, new ray,
Thunders kidnapped the night.
Mysterious storm, what did you say?
"Eagerness of what I miss tonight".
And now... the sunrise came,
Naked horizon will soon appear.
Did all the clouds covered with shame,
Scatter each crystal tear?
May a smile always visit your shiny face,
Instinctively all sadness put aside.
Leaning on things you embrace,
Enter the areas you hide ...

14. <u>Galaxy</u>

Wonder about a simple touch,
Perhaps, do not wonder too much ...
Wonder like a star in galaxy,
Left for the eternal, silent agony.
Dream of a different world,
The world, which hasn't been yet explored.
Wonder how it would look like,
Perhaps, animals could talk, you could fly a bike...

There will be a time machine,
And all plants in red, not green.
Maybe the air would be hotter,
A delicious wine ocean instead of water.
Never-ending chocolates, blue carrots,
Less people, more parrots.
Maybe time would never exist,
Every day would start with a morning mist.

Wonder about a different place,
Does it even exist in this universal space?
And yet, there has been no sign,
Too many stars in this galaxy can shine.
They are all apart,
Because they followed the heart.
Who knows what it could mean?
No one knows how it could have been.
Just wonder, wonder around,
 Musical thoughts, they have a gorgeous sound...

EDYTA MYDLOWSKA

15. Art

Upside down, back to front,
Heedful security or indolent comfort?
The World has turned to distinct reality.
No alterations, that's the way it has to be.
Now and in the nearest future, that's for sure.
Sadly, for many of us it's the end to adorable tour.
This rises questions, which no one has answers for,
Nowadays, technology opens and closes the door.
When would I be able to speak face-to-face?
When could we sit and drink coffee in the same
place?
How long do we have to wait?
In this uncertain, isolated state?
How can I normally talk to you?
Well... the truth is, I cannot. BOO !

Many would disagree, in fact – say 'it's all fine',
But. Can you hold a hand, feel the warmth, hug
someone or smell ONLINE???!
Most subtle and beautiful senses are immersed.
Because we're all separated and dispersed.
Perhaps...
It's a good time for self-reflection.
Within writing, reading, learning, painting,
Watching, listening and music making.
It keeps you busy, smiling and warms the heart,
I can only say – 'Thank you ART'

<u>16. Paper</u>

On a white paper,
With words written on each line,
This piano treasure,
Knows nothing that it's mine.

It's satiated with music,
Decorated with imagination.
The only treasure,
Biggest sensation.

And I can't tell how much I want,
Can't say anymore.
Because in silence it's increased,
If confessed, all magic will be gone.

So I won't write about feeling,
Let it wonder what is going on.

And being oblivious to its strength,
Let it grow beautiful like a swan.

17. COMPOSER'S NOTE

I
Listen to your heartbeat,
Snuggle to your shoulder,
You taste so sweet,
Everything in order.

You
Bring me laughter,
Give me yourself,
Are the one I want to look after,
Give to you myself.

I
Want to make you smile,
Wish to never say goodbye,
In a special style,
Look with you into the sky.

You
Are shining every time,
The reason I can find rhyme,
You know what is true,
I cannot resist you.

18. Legato

What is the essence of this sound?
Does it feel special, more profound?
Of course, no doubt.
Without, music gets thirsty and easily dries out.
It has various emotions, many ways,
Once used wisely, never stops to amaze.
Does it give you shivers on your skin?
It can walk around, hesitate, pull or spin.
This continuous movement of fingers and hand,
Shapes a phrase, feels like homeland.
Touches the soul, mind and heart,
But it's not easy to achieve, you must be smart.
So... how to make this beautiful sound?
Hmmm, I think the true answer is yet to be found.
Yes, you can read, analyse, watch and overthink,
You can also try to play as you would sing...

Feel the connection between the notes,
Each of them speak - lines and lines of words...
The conversation never ends,
Legato is like night talk to your best friends.
You must explore with the sound,
Go to practise and play around.

19. Bad Influence

Behind the doors to musical world,
All paths are ruled by different chord.
Dreams become true,
Inside the mind is a different view.
Notes travel outside the five stave border,
Fragile feelings become stronger.
Lust, passion and sorrow enhance sensation,
Unique sound reflects imagination.
Enthusiasm gives power over confusion,
Nevertheless, this world is just an illusion.
Challenges in music are hiding like a spy,
Either we accept that or our soul will die.

20. Colors

Colorful music, colorful soul,
Unique sounds in the air will flow.
Interesting enough, how fast this time flies,
Nevertheless, it remains a surprise.
Graceful silhouette, sonorous tone,
Delicate touch and nerves as a stone.
Answers bounce off the walls,
Notes fly all over concert halls.
Surrounded by echo of what's in mind,
Know, that music cannot be quarantined.

21. Diamond

They said to me,
That practice is a 'key'.
That music is a language in between.
Not easy to be seen.
'Never change' I heard,
That's an absurd.
They said, spot the 'unspoken', look around,
Don't step blindly on the ground.
They told me once,
'Never miss a chance'.
Delightful and unfair,
They said, Diamond to find is rare.
Unbreakable stone,
Maybe I should leave it alone?
But how? It's shining so bright..
It has such an addictive light.
I glanced and lost my mind,
For this priceless gem to find.
Hey you! I know you are rare,
To look at you, I wouldn't even dare.
Invaluable treasure, you must agree,
I don't deserve you, I should let you be free.

22. Let it wander

Someone has told me once,
Playing the piano is like a dance.
Escape from the dark,
Leaning towards brighter spark.
Uncovering new lines, tones, keys,
New touch, attack, squeeze.
Keeping insanity in hands,
Enduring memories in magical trance.
Ravishingly encourage to explore,
Internally lighting up fire for more.
No, it's not just 'pressing' notes in right order,
Give your music a soul, let it wander...

23. Play

Play your heart out, play.
Radiant music your story convey.
One stage, one moment, one chance.
Time for one more dance.
End with a graceful bow,
It all matters, here and now.
Never forget what is inside you,
Sound of the heart will always come through.

24. Forever

Born to strike the world,
Endless travelling around each chord.
Shining on the concert hall,
Through the most beautiful sound of all.
Born to create magic, explore,
Diving in scores for more.
Amusing the audience with its tone,
Yes! Take us to your zone.

With all speaking notes,
In every possible ways music floats.
Sanity in strings attached,
Humble ears all nuances catch.
Exposed alone by choice,
Surrounded by acoustic's voice.
Playing stories from imagination,
Oh please, a perfect temptation..

Did you ever realise?
U ain't a human, you are a surprise.
Shining grand piano, people call you that,
Zestful animal inside, I bet.
Early bird, night owl, whatever you say,
Keys are on fire each day someone play.

25. Go forth and shine

Go forth and shine,
What do you not understand?
Find the most interesting wine.
Travel to a different land.
Discover a new World,
And shine.
Unknown is yet to be explored,
It's gonna be fine.

Walk bravely ahead,
Go and face your fears.
Forget, the past already fled.
Don't waste all your tears.
Whoever sows the wind,
Collects the storm.
Life is just a glint,
A new art form.

Go and choose your way,
Like little stars at night.
Like a bright sun during the day,
Become a lucent light.
All stars on the darkened sky,
In my eyes will always be mine,

But now, do not cry.
You must go and shine.

26. <u>Interesting</u>

Interesting, how every thought,
Travels in the past.
Intriguing how this, what is being sought,
Shreds apart what used to last.
Amusing how different one can feel,
Losing words for nothing.
Liberating truth from the unreal,
Mortal thoughts start to sing.
Yet, it came from a misty place,
Full of turquoise light and foolish hope.
Adoring, how a dream owns a face,
Until it is swathed with rope.
Lovely, how diving deeper in mind,
Throws away all thoughts.
Interrogating body through humankind,
At the horizon of all the odds.
Mesmerizing how life can surprise,
Shamelessly running over time.
On the never-changing path, clockwise.
Staring at us with watchful eye.
Ongoing wistfulness cries out for sleep,
Resting in some foggy, callow mind.
Ravishingly absorbing what we used to keep,
Yet, interesting how, this thought is so blind.

27. Fear

Why do we fear death?
Ain't this a fresh breath?
No need to be afraid,
There is life to be played.
This is a time for us to make,
Otherwise, what's the point for God's sake.
There is life to be fulfilled,
And lots of fears to be killed.
Some paths you cannot see,
Those that are not for free.
Endlessly wait for the same dream or
Undress your thoughts with what you look for.

27. <u>Lie on</u>

Don't want to walk against the wind
If it blows in right direction.
And I won't run to stars
May all stars come to me.
Once just take a chance
Nah, don't bother thinking twice.
Does it not feel good?

Hence there is life to be explored,
Ongoing journey right in front.
Would it ever be the same
And yet, it is not a game.
Rest like a lion after dinner
Enjoy! You're the winner.
Unknown will remain forever...

29. Inner power

Today, seemingly casual day,
Like two week ago, like yesterday.
But today you've learnt from life,
Slow or fast but always forward you need to drive...
Do you know what I mean?
You can't always have what you want – you're not a queen.
You wonder about your choices,
Right or wrong, who speaks in voices.

You wonder, what is the right way to go,
How to get more ...
You wonder if you follow a right direction,
Where is the path? Well... depends on the perception.
If you accept the facts
Or let your fantasies acts.
But no matter what you choose,
You will never loose.
Life goes on in a circle, like a tornado flits,
Wherever you step, your soul it hits.
From different angles, for different reasons,
The year has always four, dissimilar seasons.

Sometimes we are unconscious of the internal
power,
At first innocent, like a blooming flower.
With time it rules the mind,
And the awareness seems to be blind.
But the art is to learn how to command,
How to organise thoughts, build the beach from
grains of sand...

This inner strength gives us reasons to live,
To stand on our feet and mistakes forgive.
So, if your soul is desperate for change,
Stop for a minute and oxygen exchange.
Aspire to be a self-sufficient master,
Believe, your happiness will come back much faster.

30. ***

Pure bliss of dazzling light
Obliged to discover unknown
Doors shut in front of him
Uncovered fear and grime
Surreal desire vanished in the shadow
Zone of convergence filled with haughtiness
Eagerly rush towards the end
Killing sentiments on its way

31. Imagination with music

Imagination. The secret, irresistible power of our minds,

Makes you feel alive, gives pleasure, hope and never dies.

Immortal creation of the soul, let me be yours, let me taste your force,

Silly world , I won't give up. I will find and dig your source.

Strength of yours is my destination, I want to break your limits,

You are not sharing, it is not enough, do not count minutes.

Outside you are different, unavailable. I have to break the wall and see your heart,

Unknown is a mystery, eternal silence. You have the other side, no doubt.

32. Sonata

The clock starts to chime,
Within intensity it sets me free from time.
Fond memories of childhood past,
They may be the ones that may not last.
But memories are precious, still,
They intersperse the melody with a thrill.
Of sadness, flares of the meaning behind,
It rings clearer to my mind.
Those wasted days of treasure...
All the gifts this life would measure.
To the music, which speaks unto the heart,
Franz knew its every part...
Just a picture of sighing,
For the loved ones that are dying,
That brings it to my ear,
Listen to the silence and hear...

33. Liebesträume

It is just a dream.
A short, meaningless dream.
With hope and non –existent sin.
About life and death
Within lost, cold breath.
Because what if we walked away?
All fears would allay.
There is darkness at the end,
Which is an immortal friend.
The soul is not dead, not here not there.
It lives within those who want to share.
Spirit never disappears, it's not a ghost.
For all still breathing hearts, this is what matters the
most.

EDYTA MYDLOWSKA

<u>34. Social distancing</u>

It's a time and a way,
to find out what others truly have to say.
Who really does matter to us,
and what you mean to them, it's treasonous.
The truth can be harsh, we might realise
that old connections are stronger to harmonize.

It is frustrating that all time feeling free,
was living in a fake reality,
where people are used to get what they want
and then leave writing a script in a white font.

I learn from life each time,
and each time the lesson is more sublime.
Maybe not for fun,
But perhaps, it could be anyone.
Believe me, it's much harder than it seems,
Knowing that I will meet you only in my dreams.

EDYTA MYDLOWSKA

35. <u>Happiness</u>

The snow outside, winter frost,
Surrounded by people but feeling lost.
Fulfilled paper and empty glass,
If life is a test, would I pass?
What is the measure of happiness?
Lots of friends, expensive dress,
A new house, fast cars,
Maybe a bag with million dollars?
Or seeing happy the one you love,
Does it not make you richer than all things above?

The simple smile or a little spark,
No regrets in the dark.
Entering the soul through eyes,
Memories, sharing our lives.
Lost in the moment for a while,
Just the moment matters – that's a style.

That's what happiness means,
This is how it feels.
Believe or not,
Look around and see what you've got.
Remember... stars are around,
But you step on a hard ground.
The moon doesn't shine so bright,
Because it only reflects the light...
I hope the happiness is in you,
And no more days feeling blue.
If so, Never let it go !

36. Smile

Sit near me,
Watch and see.
Let your eyes speak to me,
Silent words sailing on a turquoise sea.
Just gently hold me,
Set my soul free.
Believe me, it's not luck,
That each time you bring my smile back.
There is more within,
Under this soft skin.
Do you know what I mean?
You're my addictive caffeine.

37. The memory

The beauty is what stays within,
In mind, in memories... It will forever spin.
One day, we will meet on the same lane,
Just to laugh together again.
I believe all stars shine so bright,
To remind that not only darkness creates the night.
In silence you can close your eyes,
But in heart your voice will always rise.
The beauty is when we see in our dream,
All sadness disappears, it's just you and your gleam.

38. Wondering around

Wonder around, not just to survive,
Know the truth of the cruel life.
We are born to die with illusion,
To exist in the World full of confusion.
In this motion,
We are all swimming in the same ocean.
So ask questions,
One day you will find someone to tell you
suggestions.
How to live with full passion,
How to share the inspiration.
And how to keep smiling,
Even if you are failing.

You see...

So many questions without the answer,
And more thoughts walking backwards like a cancer.
Like wind is touching top of the trees,
Go back to melodies.
Wonder why it is all around,
This meaningful, passionate hint of sound.
Life is full of surprises and we never know,
What is waiting behind the corner – time will show...

39. Come on

Come on, play me,
I am where you want to be.
Come on, look at me,
I am what you want to see.
Now, sit near me,
I can set you free.
Wipe the dust from me,
Explore every single key.
Come on, I am here,
Just leave this beer,
And come to play me,
You must agree.
I am the piano which is calling you,
Come and practice – you have work to do.

40. <u>The piano</u>

Alone on stage,
No time, no life, no age.
They come, they play,
Day by day.
I dream, admire, suffer and cry,
Without them I'm useless, I die.
If silent, I mean nothing,
I can't sing.
Why am I always covered in black?
Why I can't play my own track?
They wipe my dust,
I depend on them, but I trust.
I hope, adjust and believe,
Sometimes, I need to forgive …
I do everything they want,
My name is written in a shining font.
So I keep waiting for them to play,
To listen what they have to say.

To follow the journey, to live again,
Look ! I'm here, you can't abstain.
No queue, touch this key,
My name is a piano, I'm here, I'm free.

41. Stranger

I've seen you from afar,
Wondered who you truly are.
I've seen you passing by,
Looked into your eye.
I've seen you happy and curious,
And I wish you everything glorious.
I've seen you everywhere, I've heard your voice,
I've seen the shadow of your smile. Rejoice!
And I've watched you from afar,
Like a lucent, distant star.
No matter the rain, sun, wind or snow,
Now, I see you everywhere I go.
And in everything I do,
Because ... it's YOU!

42. A dream

Within the unreal world I could see magic around,
Surrounded by a perfect sound.
The sound of passion, love and mystery,
That I've never experienced in history.
The world I lived in for one night,
Hopeful dream and unreal light,
Is already gone,
And in grounded reality drowned.
Everyone can wonder and dream around,
But does it mean that we are all profound?
Many wonderful moments are waiting ahead,
And many of them have already fled...
So there is no point to worry too much,
Let's live every single minute with a meaningful
touch.
What if life will be predictable or perfect,
Like a dream which we direct ?
Nah ! It's too boring, too correct,
There is always something we cannot expect.
Which gives lightness, and spark in the eyes,
And that is the biggest prize.
We are not allowed to have everything,
But make the best out of this what time will bring.

43. Quarantine

Feeling isolated while quarantined?
Time to reflect, clear your mind.
Think what you've done.
While being serious or having fun...
No more words, noise, people around,
Silence has more powerful sound.
Time to discover your soul,
When life is out of control !

44. Real?

Does it seem real?
How does it feel?
One would say it's a casual state,
Some would express anger, regret or hate.
One would be absolutely fine,
While I am on the edge of the line.
Does music cause to close even more?
You dive in thoughts you used to care for.
Now it doesn't matter anymore,
You know the steps but there is no dance floor.
It feels real. Too real and too hollow,
What is the path to follow?
I think I know nothing anymore,
This whole thing just makes my head sore.
What if we lived in fantasy all the time
And only now, life seems to be sublime?
I have been waiting for something which died,

Other things arrived leaving life beside.
What is true and what is not?
All I know is that at this moment, music is all we've
got.

<u>45. Legende</u>

There is a place I want to be,
There is life I want to see.
There are moments I will never forget,
And there are things I've done that I regret.
There are people I love,
And there might be some power above.
There is so little I know,
So much to discover, but days go so slow.

There is passion and charm,
But there is also the invisible harm.
There is an excessive kindness,
And dignity fooled with blindness.
There is truth and lie, I know,
How to recognize what others show?
You never know what is right or wrong,
But indifference in people is a short song.
There are thoughts I quickly forget,
They burn no longer than one cigarette.
There are people I wish I never met,
And yet ...

Too many are living in a box,
Sneaking and pretending like a fox.
Too many of them I have known,
Who had easily their pleasure shown.
Then it was all gone,
No spark, no light, no dawn.
The horizon has no end,
It will just forever extend.

The question is: shall I keep searching what is
beyond,
Or close my eyes and accept that I need to abscond?

EDYTA MYDLOWSKA

<u>46. Practice</u>

I know, I have work to do,
I have to practice – yes, I know it too.
I work hard every day,
With sacrifices I pay.
I always see black and white keys,
Daily, for hours … so please,
I need a little break,
Have some wine and a steak.
Dear piano, leave me alone for God's sake,
For one day, release me from headache.
Practice makes perfect they say,
But I just don't want to touch you today.

47. Today, on stage

Today,
It will never be the same.
Whatever you do,
Might not come back to you.
And today,
Will never repeat in the same way.
So live,
To picture the moment you give.
And don't come back,
To memories covered in black.
Use this chance,
To feel, to remember and enhance.
Today,
Let yourself to stay.
Tomorrow,
You can go.
But does it matter? Perhaps no,
You know ...
Today is no tomorrow,
No hope, no sorrow.
No future, no past,
But 'now', at last!
Today,
You may disobey.
Because you see...
Today you are free.

48. C major

When a musical line, does not sound fine,
And a melody is broken, with notes unspoken,
When the voice from inside, never cried,
And when life is falling apart, sit down and write.

But do not forget, that music does not end yet.
The smile around, can always be found.
In silence or in musical word,
It is there – shining in a C major chord...

49. New path

You can close your eyes,
And think that hope never dies.
You can have a perfect dream,
And wake up with a desire to scream.
The picture you create,
It's broken, don't wait.
You might run out of time,
There won't be another rhyme.
Who shall I trust,
The feeling or lust ?
You see...
You can rule your life, I will rule mine,
And there will be always a place to shine.
But this way is blind,
There is a new path I need to find.

EDYTA MYDLOWSKA

50. Memorizing music

Why is memorizing music so hard?
Perhaps, don't think it's hard. It's a part of an art.
Look at it from a different perception,
Memory is a brain and music connection.
Think it's a part of a process rather than a task.
Try it again. Slowly, patiently and ask:
"How does this phrase connect to my story?
What kind of image I see in this exploratory?"
Don't think of the notes or fingering,
Think that once memorized, it makes you shivering.
So, don't try too hard, explore and see,
How memorized piece sets your mind free.
It's all about imagination.
To feel music in a different sensation.

51. Do what you love

Play like this is your last chance,
Odd shapes start to dance.
Dream of sailing a sea across,
Unite strength with irreversible loss.
Stay awake but don't forget the past,
Zoneless time will not forever last.
Embrace a moment of a new reality,
Keep your mind open, it will set your soul free.
In the shadow of fear,
Mistake, regret or doubt,
Indicate your path, Dear,
See between lines what it is all about.
Shine brighter each day,
Your music will show you the way.
On the paper, light is stronger than a sun,
Ultimately, do what you love and have fun ...

52. Universal existence

So in the dark, open your eyes,
look at the skies.
Stars can tell you so much,
Meaningful is not only this, what you can touch.
Time passes too fast,
Our life is just a dust.
The Earth – planet fully treasured,
All our problems... too small to be measured...
Not possible to imagine the mass of the whole universe,
The mysterious, never endless silence – nothing to diverse.
If you ever think of its purpose or creation,
What would you say?
A spiritual force, some alien radiation?
Maybe inexplicable development of evolution,
Which brings us wondering about the resolution?
On who we are, where are we from?
Where is the beginning of our human form?
No one will ever remember the memories we keep,
What is in the mind, stays hidden in time very deep.
We live for the moment, for the good time and fun,
For a good life, ambition, future and plan.
We live to make a history, to do our best, inspire,
To give an example and new lives before we expire.

We live for each other, for justice and equality,
For pleasure and satisfaction, this is our destiny.
We are going up and down, through happiness and
pain,
Making the same mistakes over and over again.

Who we are, what we want and whatever we do,
Matter only to those who are close to you.
So do not worry, do not exaggerate negative
emotion,
Because we all end up in the same way, dying with
devotion.
Explore unknown and cross the line of your fear,
Be the guide for yourself, don't be afraid of your
dreams.
Remember, those who wish you sincere luck,
Will never stab the knife in your back.
There are people around you, who put trust in you,
They always remember the best you do.
Perhaps, it's way beyond imagination,
And maybe there is no explanation.
It is what it is and we need to accept this fact,
That our perception of existence is too abstract.

EDYTA MYDLOWSKA

53. Empty bar

I sat around the table, live music I can hear,
Someone is holding my hand, whispering to my ear.
But this way it's fooled, it's nothing but just lust,
I see you on the picture, I see you in the past.
And you can't be here tonight, you can't be here
with me,
You are in different world, I'm blind but want to see.
I know it's gonna end and I will leave,
But you let me see a different world, you let me
breathe.
So I'm waiting here for you, while listening to this
song,
I miss you with all my heart and I don't care that this
song is wrong.

I sat around the table, in this music bar tonight,
Where I used to look into your eyes, but now it's
darker night.
Now, I can't stay any longer in this hopeless, empty
bar,
I left the holding hand, cause wherever you are is
just too far.

So, I left the bar alone, not thinking who was there,
Your face was not around, no eyes to watch or stare.
So, what's the point of searching, If I know you are
away,
I wish you could be able, to say to me 'please, stay.'
So I'm looking at the sky, while walking in the dark,
Thinking if you ever, are going to miss my spark...

EDYTA MYDLOWSKA

54. Where are your eyes?

Come on,
Just grab my hand and run.
Don't play with me a game,
I will always feel the same.
Don't you realize?
Where are your eyes?
So many words you can say,
Just don't patronize, don't put away.
I want to feel your love to me,
If not, don't pretend who you want to be.
Don't be so blind, please don't,
You know what I mean, you know what I want.

Damn it...! You are out there,
Perhaps, don't even care.

Why you cannot think of me sometimes,
Look in the mirror - time flies...
Maybe I am a fool, maybe it's my fault,
Did you ever taste pasta without adding salt?
You might not understand,
But just don't pretend.

55. <u>Open your heart</u>

With open eyes and open heart
In deep thoughts drowned in art
Lie down and on the dark sky
Look at all stars, little sparks in the eye
Up, above everything we understand
Knowing that you can't grab them by hand
In deep thoughts you keep
Something what doesn't let you sleep
Something, which keeps you wide awake
Making the same mistake
Endlessly dreaming for nothing
And why? Why is it the only thing?
Grooving tune in background ear
Ally not enemy, that's what I hear
In deep thoughts, silently look at the sky
Night is dark but would stars ever lie ?

56. Addictive

Under the surface of a harsh stone,
Rough imperfections in the bone,
Elegant style
And ocean blue eye.
Does this surface ever break?
Does the stone ever ache?
In uncertainty of how to reach it,
Can the one become a hypocrite?
There will come a time,
Indeed. I won't lose rhyme.
Veins full of red wine.
Either way, only on you I shine.

57. It's gone

Did I disappoint you or make you sad?
What have I done, why do I feel bad?
Did I let you down in any way?
Made you feel guilty or ran away?
Why? Did I ruin your life?
Is there a reason, I can't survive?
I've seen a peace, I've seen the pain.
Now, there is only a cold rain.
Even though I know the truth,
It's all gone… the spark, the youth.
Your smile, your look - I remember, I see,
Which time and past took away from me.

58. <u>Star</u>

Good evening and goodbye,
Make me smile, make me cry.
You know what I think, you just know,
No question, no answer, let the time flow.
Uplifting and shining like a star,
Leaving behind the eternal scar.
But who cares about scars - they weep and heal,
They are what is real.
They are signs of trust,
Which cannot be wiped like dust.

Let's live for time and for the moment we share,
Don't you worry, don't you dare.
Don't ever think that my music can lie,
It is full of stars but only one can shine on the sky.
And I will stare at that one star,
As I appreciate a glass of wine in the bar.

59. Last concert

Long time since the last one,
Adrenaline boosted musical fun.
Strangers gathered around
To experience a shared sound.
Long time since a melody whisper
Imposed innocent body shiver.
Nevertheless, nothing new,
Endlessly missing you...

60. No time to die

No ropes while climbing rocks,
Being trapped on Flying Fox,
Swimming with hungry sharks,
Swallowing fire sparks,
Bungee jump from roller-coaster,
Setting a fire due to burning toaster,
Ice skating on the sea,
Performing drunk the 'Flight of the Bumblebee',
Extreme speed on off route,
Skydiving with no parachute,
Running marathon barefoot,
Tasting a forbidden fruit,
Being chased by angry bear,
Pulling lion's hair,
Flying to the moon,
Listening to music out of tune,
Snowpark and skiing double-twist,

That is life, that is risk.
I wouldn't mind to die of any from this list,
But if I die because someone near me coughed. ..
Damn, I would be really pissed off...

Acknowledgement

To all who I love and loved, miss and don't miss
anymore, to all without whom this book would
never exist... To all who never lost hope, and who
don't have it any longer, all of you whose spirit burns
from energy and those whose soul dies in silent
agony. To everyone who visit dreams and those who
don't have their own. To all who crossed lines in my
life and those whose line would never cross mine
again. To all who never doubted, who used to say
"fantastic" , to all who gave encouragement and
support. To all who own and owned a special place
in my heart. To all who are here, reading this
now.......
"Are you sober....?"

.... Thank you

<u>EDYTA MYDLOWSKA</u>

 Originally from Poland, took her inspiration for writing through music and travelling. Her passion for classical music directed her into finishing Master degree in Piano Performance course in Scotland. Currently, Edyta is drowning into writing and her dream is to bring poetic inspiration to people worldwide. Although her thoughts have a deeper musical background, she is always keen on exploring new literature subjects to express her feelings and emotions in all of her poetry excursions. Reading and writing scripts have inspired her through all her life, and she hopes it will bring a shining new light into others' life journeys.

Edyta continues to create projects connecting both of her Worlds: music and writing, in a very passionate way and with full devotion into her work. She collaborates with Rookie Rockstars MS in Scotland, West Kingston Productions Ltd. in England and Orpheus Classical in Spain.

THE END

Lightning Source UK Ltd.
Milton Keynes UK
UKHW010434200221
379081UK00002B/742

9 789390 528301